ENHANCED MENTAL HEALTH

Terms and Conditions

Table of Contents

Foreword

When you hear the term "emotional health or mental health", what is the first thing that usually comes into your mind? According to researches, mental health normally includes social well-being pertaining to psychological and emotional standings. Mental health affects the way people think, act and feel. In addition to this, mental health also has the ability to help you determine the effective ways of how to handle your stress, make choices and relate to other people.

Mental health is essential in each stage of your life, from childhood, adolescence and adulthood. For those people who are experiencing mental health issues and problems, there is a great chance that your behavior, mood and thinking will be affected. There are different factors that usually contribute to your mental health issues and problems such as family history, life experiences that include abuse and trauma and biological factors that include brain chemistry and genes.

It is a fact that mental health issues and problems are very common however help and prevention is always available. People who are suffering from mental health issues and problems have a great chance to get better and recover completely. For those individuals who are experiencing mental health issues and problems, it is very imperative that you are familiar and aware about the warning signs of having mental health issues and problems. If you have positive and effective mental health, it will allow you to make meaningful contributions to your community, work productively, cope with stress and realize your full potential.

In addition to this, it is also important that you have an apparent and superior understanding about the effective and useful ways of how you can maintain your positive and effective mental health such as developing your coping skills, getting enough hours of sleep, helping others, getting physically fit and active, staying positive, connecting with other people and most importantly getting professional advice and help from experts.

Enhanced Mental Health

Chapter 1:

Synopsis

According to studies, individuals who are emotionally and mentally healthy have the ability to control their behavior and emotions. They also have the capability to handle life trials and challenges, recover from serious seatbacks and build strong and healthy relationships with others. However, you need to bear in mind that if you want to maintain or build emotional health, mental health and physical health, effort, commitment, time and dedication is highly recommended.

It is true that enhancing your mental and emotional health is a rewarding experience that you will definitely love. Mental health can benefit all the salient aspects of your life such as adding enjoyment to your day to day activities, building resilience and most importantly boost your mood.

For those people who are experiencing emotional health or mental health problems, it is very important that they are familiar and aware about how to get rid of it in just a short period of time. Here, you will learn the real definition and significance of emotional health and mental health.

A Quick Glimpse to Emotional Health or Mental Health

Emotional or mental health usually refers to your overall psychological being. It also includes your ability to manage your emotions and feelings, build relationships, develop the way you look and feel about yourself and most importantly how you can deal with extreme difficulties. Mental health is not just about the absence of mental health issues and problems.

Being emotionally and mentally healthy is more than being free of psychological issues, anxiety and depression. The absence of emotional and mental health commonly refers to the presence of excellent characteristics.

There are some people who don't have negative emotions and feelings however they still need to do things that will make them feel good and positive to help them get a hold on their emotional and mental health. Individuals who are emotionally and mentally healthy have the following:

✓ High self esteem and self confidence

✓ They have the ability to maintain and build fulfilling relationships

✓ They have a balance between their play, work, activity, rest and a lot more

✓ They have the flexibility to know and learn new things and at the same time they can easily adapt it to change

✓ They have a great sense of purpose and meaning in their relationships and activities

✓ They have the ability to easily and effectively deal with life challenges and stress and bounce back from adversity

✓ They have the ability to have fun and laugh as well as they have zest for living

✓ People who are emotionally and mentally healthy have a great sense of tranquility and contentment.

The positive characteristics of emotional and mental health will allow you to easily participate in all the latest happenings in your life by having strong relationships, meaningful activities and being productive every single day. The effective and positive characteristics of emotional and mental health will greatly help you to quickly cope with life stresses, trials and challenges.

Warning Signs of Having Emotional or Mental Health Problems

Not all people are familiar and aware about the warning signs of having emotional or mental health issues and problems. For those people who want to know and learn about the warning signs of having emotional and mental health issues and problems, just check this out:

- Inability to execute daily activities and tasks such as getting to school or work and taking care of your family and kids

- Thinking of harming other people and yourself

- Believing things or hearing voices that are not real

- Having persistent memories and thoughts that you can't easily get out of your mind

- Experiencing mood swings that can cause major problems in your relationships

- Fighting and yelling with friends and family

- Feeling unusually scared, worried, upset, angry, forgetful and confused

- Using drugs, drinking and smoking

- Feeling hopeless and helpless

- Having unexplained pains and aches

- Feeling numb

- Having no energy

- Pulling away from your usual activities and people

- Sleeping and eating too little or too much

Mental Wellness and Health

According to studies, positive and good mental health allows you to:

- Make evocative contributions to your community

- Work productively

- Cope with pressure and stress in life

- Realize your full potential

Effective Ways to Build and Maintain Positive and Better Mental Health

- Developing your coping skills

- Get accurate hours of sleep

- Helping other people

- Getting physically fit and active

- Staying positive

- Connecting with other people

- Getting professional guidance, advice and help especially if your need it

It is a fact that emotional and mental health issues and problems are quite common in different parts of the world. According to researches, many American adults experience mental health problems. In addition to this, young people also experience major depression and some Americans live with serious mental problem that includes depression, bipolar disorder and schizophrenia. Moreover, suicide is considered as the top notch cause of major death in Unites States of America.

Chapter 2:

Are you Resilient?

Synopsis

Being mentally and emotionally healthy does not mean that you are not going to experience bad times or emotional problems. Most people go through change, loss and disappointments. These are considered as normal parts of your life however they can still cause stress, anxiety and sadness. The only difference is that people who are emotionally and mentally healthy have the ability to bounce back from stress, trauma and adversity. This type of ability is known as *resilience*.

Individuals who are mentally and emotionally healthy have the helpful tools that are intended for coping with difficult scenarios in life and at the same time maintain and build a positive outlook on life. These people remain creative, flexible and focused during the bad times of their lives. One of the best key factors of resilience is your ability to completely balance your emotions and stress. If you have the potential to recognize your feelings and emotions, you can be sure that you will find hard times and difficulties much easier to cope and deal with effectively and appropriately.

By doing this, you are assured that you can avoid getting stuck in a negative mood or suffering from anxiety and depression. Another important key factor is having an excellent support network. If you have trusted people that you can turn to during bad times and hardships in life, you can easily find support and encouragement that will boost your resilience during tough times. Here, you will discover the role of resilience in emotional and mental health.

Physical Health is simply Connected to Emotional and Mental Health

It is a fact that taking good care of yourself is considered to be a powerful way to get a hold on your emotional and mental health. Your body and mind are linked together and this is one of the reasons why when you develop your physical health, you will automatically experience greater emotional and mental well-being.

Regular exercise will not just strengthen your lungs and heart, it also has the potential to release endorphins within your body. Endorphins are powerful chemicals that are responsible for energizing the body as well as lifting the mood of people. Daily choices as well as the activities that you engage in can greatly affect the way you feel emotionally and physically.

Tips on how to Get a Hold on Your Emotional and Mental Health

If you are a person who wants to easily get a hold on their emotional and mental health, it is very imperative that you are familiar and aware of some very effective tips. The following are some tips that will make getting a hold on your mental health much easier.

Have enough rest- In order to maintain good emotional and mental health, the first thing that you need to do is to take good care of yourself, especially your body. Having enough rest and getting adequate hours of sleep is highly recommended, especially with teenagers. Individuals need 7-8 hours of sleep every night to function optimally. If you have enough hours of sleep, you can be sure that you are one step closer to becoming emotionally and mentally healthy.

✓ **Learn good nutrition-** You need to learn how to have a well-balanced diet. A lot of people are unaware of how large of a role nutrition actually plays in our moods and our mental health. It may be difficult for you to follow this diet in the beginning but it will surely pay off in the long run.

✓ **Exercise to get rid of stress-** It is a fact that regular exercise has the ability to help you to easily get rid of stress and at the same time it can lift up your mood. According to studies, exercise is considered to be a powerful antidote for depression, anxiety and stress. You can look for simple ways that you can add exercise into your daily activities such as taking the stairs of your house instead of using the elevator or you can also go on short walks. If you want to experience the amazing benefits of being emotionally and mentally healthy, 30 minutes of daily exercise can be a great help.

✓ **Get a small dose of sunlight each day-** Sunlight has the ability to lift your mood. The best thing that you can do is to get a small dose of sunlight each day for about 10-15 minutes. This can also be done while you are socializing, gardening and exercising.

✓ **Limit your Alcohol intake-** Apart from drinking alcohol, it is also important to avoid using drugs and cigarettes. These are well known stimulants that have the ability to let your feel good for a short period of time, however they have long term negative effects, especially for your emotional health and mood.

Being resilient does not cost anything and anyone can master it, especially with the presence of practice. Most of all, being resilient has the ability to enhance every aspect of your life.

Chapter 3:

Take Good Care of Yourself

Synopsis

For those individuals who want to improve, strengthen and maintain their emotional and mental health, the first thing that they can do is to take good care of their selves. It is very essential to pay attention to your feelings and needs. Don't let negative emotions and stress build up in your system since it can harm your overall health. You have to balance the things that you love to do and your daily activities and responsibilities. If you take good care of yourself, you can be sure that you are a hundred percent prepared and ready to deal with trials and challenges that might come into your life. Taking good care of yourself usually includes pursuing the activities that release endorphins within your body. According to researchers, endorphins are naturally released within your body when you do the following:

- **Positively impact others-** It is a fact that being valued for all the things that you do and being useful to other people can easily build self-confidence and self-esteem. If you really want to build your self-confidence and self-esteem, do certain things that can greatly impact other people in a nice and meaningful way.

- **Practice the importance of self-discipline-** It is true that self control can lead to a sense of hopefulness and at the same time it can greatly help you to easily overcome your negative thoughts, helplessness and despair. By practicing self-discipline, you can be sure that you can easily become emotionally and mentally healthy.

- **Enjoy the wondrous beauty of art and nature-** There are some studies that show that by simply walking in your garden, you can reduce your stress and lower down the level of your blood pressure. Apart from this, sitting on a beach, viewing architecture, hiking and strolling through art galleries and parks can also lower your blood pressure and reduce stress.

- **Manage your level of stress-** According to researchers, stress takes a heavy toll on people's emotional and mental health. This is one of the reasons why you need to manage and control your stress. It is a fact that not all stressors can be easily prevented however strategies for stress management will greatly help you to bring things into balance.

- **Limit your unhealthy emotional and mental habits-** Too much worrying is considered as one of the well known unhealthy emotional and mental habits of most people in the present time. It is very important to avoid becoming too absorbed by your repetitive mental habits. Moreover, negative thoughts can suck up your time and drain your energy. It can also trigger your feelings of depression, fear and anxiety.

Helpful and Effective Strategies and Tips for Taking Good Care of yourself

In order to become emotionally and mentally healthy, it is very significant that you have an apparent and better understanding about the helpful and effective strategies for taking good care of yourself. Check this out:

✓ **Appeal on your senses-** Stay energized and calm by simply appealing on your five senses such as taste, smell, touch, sound and sight. You can listen to your favorite music to easily lift up your mood. You can also place a bounce of flowers on your patio where you can smell and see them. You can also massage your feet and hands or you can also sip your favorite warm drink.

✓ **Engage in creative and meaningful work-** You can execute things that will greatly challenge your superior creativity. By doing this, you can be sure that you feel more productive every single day. You can engage yourself in gardening, playing an instrument, writing, drawing or even building your own workshop. By doing this, you can completely explore your strengths and weaknesses.

✓ **Get a pet-** It is a fact that pets are a big responsibility however caring for a pet will make you feel loved and needed. Your pet can also serve as your buddy. You will also need to take your pet for a walk and this will cause you to exercise and meet new people.

✓ **Make your leisure time a priority-** If you are doing things for no reason, it simply means that you are happy and contented while doing them. Spend your leisure time with exciting and memorable activities such as a walk on the beach, reading amazing books, chatting with your friends, listening to your favorite music and watching a funny movie. It is true that playing is considered to be a mental and emotional health necessity.

✓ **Make time for your appreciation and contemplation-** The first thing that you can do is to think of all the wondrous things that you are grateful for. You can pray, meditate, enjoy watching the beautiful sunset or spend time paying attention to what is beautiful, positive and good as you continue the rest of the day.

Everyone is different and not all things will be beneficial to all people. There are some individuals who prefer to relax while some want to have more activities to enjoy and explore.

Chapter 4:

Healthy Relationships

Synopsis

It is true that healthy and supportive relationships are recognized as the foundation of mental and emotional health. No matter how much effort and time that you devote in improving your emotional and mental health, you still need the help others and it will make your feel great about yourself. According to studies, humans are considered to be social creatures with a mental need for positive connections and relationships with others. Social brains of humans usually crave for companionship. Social interaction with other people provides an opportunity to express the issues you are having which can reduce stress.

The ultimate key that you need to find is a healthy and supportive relationship with someone who is perfect and a good listener. Find someone that you can talk to every day and who will listen to your agenda and life problems. A perfect and good listener will listen to your feelings and won't judge, criticize or interrupt you. If you really want to find a good listener, the first thing that you can do is to become a good listener too.

Develop a friendship with someone you can talk every day, listen to your life problems and challenges and support you without asking in return. Here, you will learn some important strategies and tips for connecting to other people without encountering any difficulties and hassles.

Discover the Essential Strategies and Tips for Connecting to other People

When it comes to healthy relationships, it is very important that you have a clear and superior understanding about the salient strategies and tips that will greatly help you to easily connect to other people. With the help of these strategies and tips, you are assured that you can easily find someone who can listen and accompany you during your hardships in life.

✓ **Get out from behind your Computer and TV Screen**

Computers and TVs can offer their own form of companionship and can be a stress reliever however they do not compare to interactions with other people. This is one of the reasons why you don't need to neglect the real world healthy relationships in favor of your virtual interaction.

✓ **Spend more time with people you like to talk and deal with**

It is very important to give more time to people you like to talk and deal with. Choose colleagues, family members, neighbors and friends who are positive, upbeat and interested in you. Take ample time to inquire about the people you meet and know more things about them.

✓ **Volunteer**

Doing things that will help other people has an excellent effect on how you normally feel about yourself. The purpose and meaning you find in helping other people will expand and enrich your life. Charitable organizations, non-profits, churches and schools usually depend on volunteers for their survival.

✓ **Be an excellent joiner**

It is highly recommended to join interest groups, conversations, social actions and networks that will give you a great chance to meet different ranges of people. These groups usually offer wondrous opportunities for finding various people with common likes and interests. Those people who you like to talk to and deal with are recognized as your potential friends.

The Perks of Healthy and Supportive Relationships

Strong and healthy relationships are essential to your healthy life and happiness. Individuals with perfect and good friendships have the ability to handle stress. It is very important to find a friend who will help you during hardships in life. One of the best and effective ingredients of healthy and strong relationships is honest and open communication.

Work together to easily build and create a strong environment wherein both of you can feel secure and safe while expressing your dreams, hopes and feelings with one another. Here are some of the excellent communication skills that you need to enhance to come up with great results. Check this out:

- **Empathy**

  This is considered as the ability to express and understand the interest of one another. It does not mean that you need to easily agree with it, all you need to do is to acknowledge it and at the same time try to understand. By doing this, you can show to them that you truly care.

- **Acceptance**

You need to recognize that you don't have the ability to make your friend change. It is very important to take responsibility for your own actions, attitudes and feelings. Trying to change your friend into the person you want them to be will not work. You can build strong and healthy relationships when you know the main purpose of acceptance.

- **Valuing others**

You need to bear in mind that most people want to be loved, valued and appreciated. It is very imperative to pay attention to your interactions with friends. Let them feel that they are valued and important. In this way building healthy relationships is one step closer to you.

- **Listening**

The last thing that you need to bear in mind, especially if you want to get a hold of a healthy and supportive relationship is to be a good listener. If you are chatting with your friends or family members, make it a habit to have eye to eye contact and an open posture. Avoid crossing your legs and arms. Before giving your opinion, allow them to finish their stories.

If you have these effective communication skills, you can be sure that you can easily acquire the strong and healthy relationships that you are seeking for.

Chapter 5:

Synopsis

Emotional and mental health continues to shape your life experiences. Early experiences during your childhood are really important. Biological and genetic factors play a significant role in your life however these two factors can also be changed by your life experiences.

The Risk Factors

If you want to get a hold of a better mind, better life and better living, it is very essential that you are familiar and aware about the risk factors that have the ability to compromise emotional and mental health. Here are some of the risk factors that can compromise your emotional and mental health.

- **Poor attachment and connection to your primary caretaker in life-** Feeling abused, confused, unsafe, isolated and lonely as a young child or infant.

- **Serious losses and Traumas in life-** Traumatic experiences that include hospitalization or war as well as sudden death of parents.

- **Learned Helplessness-** Negative experiences and situations in life that usually lead to a certain belief can make you feel helpless. This is one of the reasons why you need to have control over the latest situations and happenings in your life.

- **Illness-** This is considered as one of the risk factors that can affect your emotional and mental health especially when your illness is chronic, isolates and disables you from other people.

- **Side effects of your medications-** This kind of risk factors usually happens to older people who are taking different types of medications for their illness and diseases. The side effects of their medications can compromise their emotional and mental health.

- **Substance Abuse-** It is a fact that drug and alcohol abuse can cause emotional and mental health issues and problems. This can also make your mental health get worse.

Whatever external and internal factors have shape your emotional and mental health, it is not too late for you to change and improve your psychological well-being. It is true that risk factors can be easily counteracted with effective protective factors such as coping strategies, healthy lifestyles and strong relationships for managing negative emotions and stress.

For those people who are encountering emotional and mental health issues and problems, the best thing that they can do is to immediately consult a professional psychiatrist who will greatly help them to regain their emotional and mental health. Aside from this, you can also try stress management techniques, healthy lifestyles, supportive and healthy relationships and coping emotional strategies that will serve as your key and guide to easily bring back your emotional and mental health.

However if all your efforts did not work out, it simply means that this is the best time for you to consult a professional and reliable psychiatrist who will provide you with help, advice and guidance on how you can easily cope with your normal life. There are various psychiatrists who specialize in the field of regaining emotional and mental health. They are the ones that you should consult and rest assured that they will greatly help you in bringing back your normal.

Chapter 6:

When Do You Need to See a Professional?

Synopsis

If you already made all your efforts just to enhance your emotional and mental health, but still don't feel good, it is the perfect time for you to seek professional help. Since most people are socially attuned, input from a reliable, knowledgeable and competent caring professional can motivate you to do things that will help you to regain your emotional and mental health. Here, you will discover the red flag behaviors and feelings that require immediate attention. Check this out:

Red Flag Behaviors and Feelings of Having Emotional and Mental Health Problems

- Thoughts of suicide and death

- Self destructive and negative thoughts and fears that you can't immediately control

- Using alcohol, drugs, food and nicotine to cope during hardships in line and difficult situations

- Concentration problems that can interfere with your home and work life

- Feeling helpless, hopeless and down throughout the day

- Inability to have enough sleep

If you notice that you have these red flag symptoms, the best thing that you can do is to set an appointment with your professional psychiatrist or emotional health professional. There is a wide variety of emotional health specialist and professionals who will greatly help you to easily get rid of your emotional and mental health issues and problems. It is very important that you choose the elite mental health specialist to make sure that you can come up with the best results. It is a fact that selecting the superb emotional health professional is not an easy task to do since it requires intensive research, time, commitment and dedication to obtain great results but it will be well worth it.

Emotional and mental health issues and problems have corresponding solutions. It should be treated ahead of time to keep it from getting worse. If you have loved ones who are experiencing emotional and mental health issues and problems, it is highly recommended to immediately seek professional help from mental health specialists and psychiatrists. They are the ones who can provide them with appropriate and effective therapy and medication that will help them to easily regain their normal life. However, don't forget to try some of the helpful strategies and techniques to control emotional and mental health issues and problems.

Seeking professional help from experts as soon as possible can help patients to easily recover from their situations. It is true that emotional and mental health problems are a serious health conditions that need proper attention and medication. If their condition is not properly attended, there is a great chance that symptoms will get worse and treating them will require a long duration of time. If you want to have a better mind, better life and better living, this is the best time for you to take good care of your emotional and mental health. Being emotionally and mentally healthy will greatly help you to execute your daily activities perfectly and effectively.

www.ingramcontent.com/pod-product-compliance
Lightning Source LLC
Chambersburg PA
CBHW040057240726
48664CB00004B/1230